AF374799

First Edition

Published by Julia Fonti.
Printed in the United States of America.
Illustrations are generated with Midjourney AI and edited by Julia Fonti.

To the Parents

It is a trip to be a parent;
I wish kids' needs were more apparent.
We read so many clever books,
To understand their acts and looks.

The hardest journey, filled with hope,
Limitless love, and no days off,
Through sleepless nights, and joyful days,
We loose ourselves in a wondrous maze.

Though there is no recipe for all,
To raise them well's a tricky goal.
I hope with help from magic keys,
You'll better understand your kids.

Unlock the powers of compassion,
Embrace all feelings with affection,
Be generous with your attention,
And live with only joy to mention!

- Julia

by Julia Fonti
Keys For Kids' Needs

For Evan, Josephine & William

With gentle words I'll show you way,
To grow and thrive, to learn and play,
Together strong we rise above,
Unlocking peace – the key is Love!

Love Key

When boo-boo hurts and miss you lots,
When day is rough and task is tough,
When nothing seems to be enough,
We all could use the key of love!

With love we find a way through fears,
It wipes away the hardest tears.
With every hug and every cheer,
I promise to be always near.

I love you unconditionally,
I'm always here to guide
and support you.

It is ok to make mistakes,
And feel so angry, too.
I am right here, I feel and hear,
And I'll always be with you.

My love is pure, strong and true,
Let's hug it out and talk things through,
To solve a problem or make things right,
We do the best when we unite.

I love you!

When you frown, upset with me,
Shouting loud and endlessly,
I stay calm and let you be,
Then use the key of Empathy.

Empathy Key

Shouting, throwing things around,
You feel ignored and wronged.
You want a toy, a screen, a treat,
The world is shaking underneath your feet.

I listen close and take my time,
To understand what's on your mind.
I help you find the words to say,
And guide you gently through the fray.

I understand your feelings,

and I'm here to help you

through whatever you're experiencing.

It is okay to ask for things,
You're heard & understood.
And one by one, I'll give you all,
When time is right and good.

I'll always listen & respect,
I'll comfort & explain,
And every argument we have,
Will never be in vain.

I understand you!

14

So lucky is for you & me,
That mommy has a Patience key.
I'll soothe your heart when things get tough,
With gentle words and tender love.

Patience Key

Your body like a magic shelf,
Keeps all the feelings in itself.
And they are hard to hold inside,
As feelings tend to grow in size.

But when they storm and overflow,
It's time to let those feelings show.
With patience and our minds so clear,
We face them all without fear.

I'll be patient with you

as you learn and grow,

no matter how long it takes.

When we feel angry, wronged or hurt,
It's very hard to think.
Bad things can happen if we act
Faster than we blink.

There is no self that cannot shelf
That energy within,
Life is precious – let's be patient
And let the patience win!

I am always

here for you!

18

If only I could know all things
The best of moms should know,
The key of an Apology
Would never need to show!

Apology Key

Sometimes it seems the up is down,
No matter what we do.
First bad behavior, then lying,
First "Mama, I hate You!'

To be a parent is not easy -
That is what people say.
We are in search of an advice,
Get lost along the way.

I'm sorry if I made you feel upset,

I'll do my best to listen

and improve.

A humble heart and softened tone
Can mend what's gone awry,
The key is in apology,
To calm the tide inside.

Through understanding we can heal,
We learn from every fall.
Only kindness in parent's guidance
Can help a child grow tall.

I am sorry I hurt
your feelings!

When You get bored as can be,
I reach for my Attention key.
With games and stories fun to share,
To spark your joy and show I care.

Attention Key

With kindness, love, a bit of patience,
I praise my child with attention.
Watch, listen, seek to understand,
Use gentle words or lend a hand.

Set work aside, I stay awhile,
Play tag, do craft, share a smile.
Create some memories, spend time together,
And wish this day would last forever!

I'm fully present with you,

giving you my time and attention

because you matter.

I bet it's hard to be a child:
To wonder what the world's about,
To understand what's right and wrong,
And navigate where you belong.

And when there is no one to help,
It's no surprise you start to yelp.
Yet every minute that we share,
Fills up your chest with love and care.

I love spending

time with you!

There's no one else I'd rather be,
Than who I am, when you are with me.

I hope you feel with me the same,
And we can read this book again!

The End

Let's Talk!

What are some ways to show love?

Do you feel respected by me?

What does make you feel loved the most?

What is empathy?

What is the appropriate thing to do when someone is angry with us?

Is it important to be a patient person?

What is the appropriate thing to say when someone apologizes to us?

How do you get someone's attention when they are busy?

What is your favorite activity?

What do you think if we could schedule a
10 minutes play time together every day?

Let's Think!

Love is the answer. - Albert Einstein, physicist

Be kind, for everyone you meet is fighting a hard battle. - Socrates, philosopher

Patience is the sister of success. - Aristotle, philosopher

Saying sorry is an act of courage. - Bruce Lee, Kong fu master

Give work your attention, and you'll only have to do it once. - Julia Fonti, writer

About the author

Julia was born in Logoisk, Minsk region, Belarus, and began writing at the age of 12, winning multiple awards for poetry and songwriting. At 19, she immigrated to the United States and made San Francisco her home for the next 14 years. Although she initially wrote primarily in Russian, she put her writing and singing career on hold to pursue a path in Art and Exhibition design.

She worked for a San Francisco-based company, first as an Art Dealer and later as an Artist Liaison. For the past seven years, Julia has been a full-time mom to her three children, two dogs, and two ducks.

Today she lives in Colorado, and is making her return to the writing world with a charming and educational children's book for parents.

Thank You!

www.juliafonti.com